CONTENTS

INTRODUCTION

Systems of Life has been running for almost 20 years and it continues to be a firm favourite with *Nursing Times'* readers. The collected volumes, of which this is the third, are also proving to be enormously popular.

The success of the feature depends, we believe, on two factors. First, nurses, students, tutors and other health professionals need regular and easy access to sound, reliable updates on anatomy and physiology. Second, the clear, attractive illustrations and highly readable text of Systems of Life make that updating a pleasure rather than a chore.

The series is put together by a team of three: writer, Anne Roberts; illustrator, Peter Gardiner and desk editor, Jean Cullinan. Between them, they bring to the task a wealth of experience and an assured touch. I hope you will find their latest offering both useful and enjoyable.

John Gilbert
Editor, *Nursing Times*

THE EYE AND VISION

The eyes take in visual information from the outside world and transmit it to the brain.
The eyeball is hollow and almost spherical. Its wall has three layers: sclera, choroid and retina.

The choroid is the middle coat, containing pigment granules and many blood vessels.

The inner layers of the choroid form the ciliary body, pleated into ciliary processes overlying the ciliary muscles.

Anteriorly the outer layers of the choroid form the iris, a circular diaphragm; the pigment here gives the eye its colour, and the coloured iris rings the space called the pupil.

The sclera is a tough, fibrous, complete coat which holds the eyeball together.

The posterior five-sixths is white and opaque, and part of this is visible from the front as the 'white of the eye'.

The anterior one-sixth of the sclera forms the transparent cornea.

Lens

The anterior chamber is the space between the cornea and the iris.

The posterior chamber

The optic nerve is a continuation of the retina, leaving the eye at the blind spot and running to the brain.

The lens of the eye in its elastic capsule is attached to the ciliary processes by suspensory ligaments.

Behind the lens is the vitreous humour. This jelly-like mass forms a hyaline membrane peripherally, and is condensed in front to form the suspensory ligament of the lens.

The retina is the inner coat of the eye. Its outer pigment layer lies against the choroid, and the inner, nervous layer is sensitive to light.

The posterior chamber lies between the iris and the lens.
Both the anterior and posterior chambers contain aqueous humour.

Light enters the eye through the cornea and is focused on the retina by the transparent structures it passes through:
the cornea, the aqueous humour, the lens and the vitreous humour.
Visual information passes from the retina to the brain along the optic nerve;
in the brain it is interpreted, compared with memory stores and retained for future reference.

The eyeball lies in the bony eye-socket, the orbit, which protects it from injury.
The brain is immediately above the orbital roof, while the nasal cavity and ethmoid and sphenoidal sinuses lie medially.
The maxillary air sinus is beneath its floor.

There are six extrinsic or external eye muscles, which rotate the eyeball within the orbit.
Together they form an incomplete cone shape around and behind it.
There are: four straight muscles, the superior, inferior, medial and lateral recti;
two oblique muscles, superior and inferior.

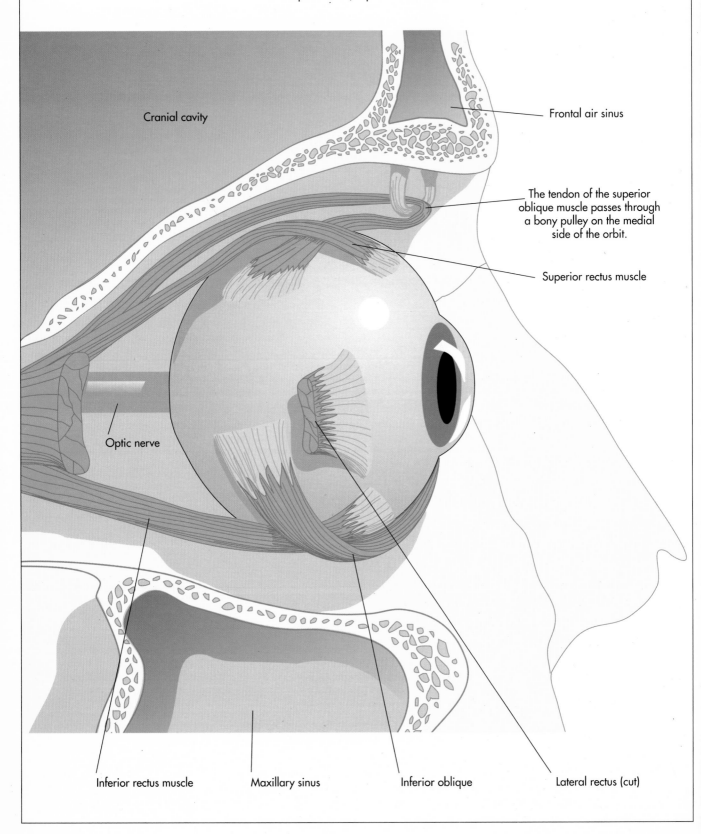

Cranial cavity

Frontal air sinus

The tendon of the superior oblique muscle passes through a bony pulley on the medial side of the orbit.

Superior rectus muscle

Optic nerve

Inferior rectus muscle

Maxillary sinus

Inferior oblique

Lateral rectus (cut)

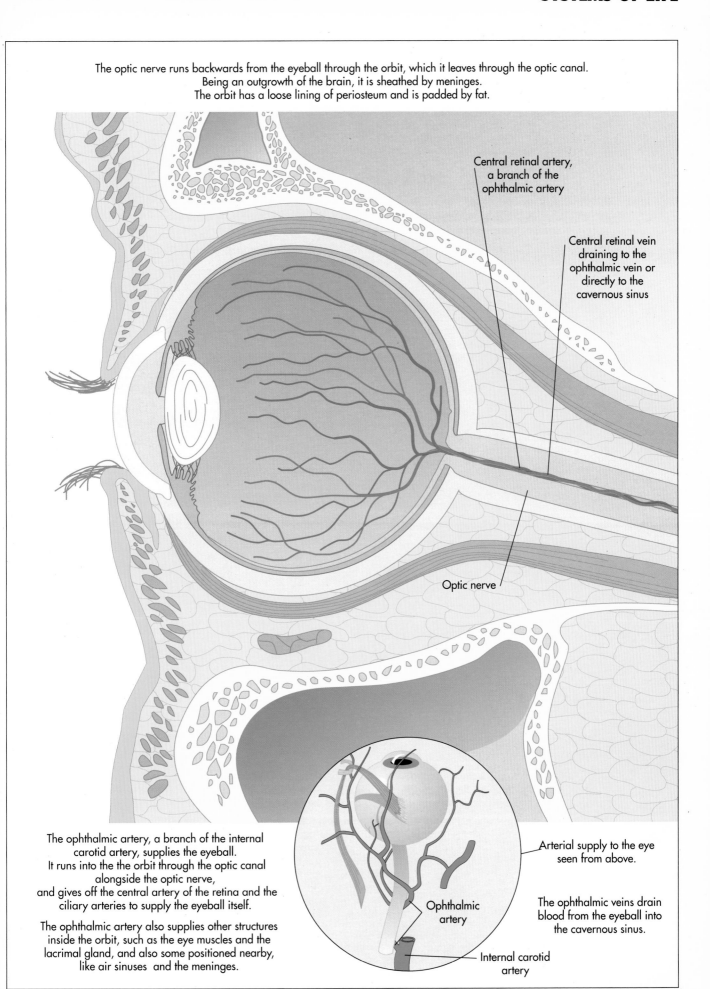

The optic nerve runs backwards from the eyeball through the orbit, which it leaves through the optic canal.
Being an outgrowth of the brain, it is sheathed by meninges.
The orbit has a loose lining of periosteum and is padded by fat.

Central retinal artery, a branch of the ophthalmic artery

Central retinal vein draining to the ophthalmic vein or directly to the cavernous sinus

Optic nerve

The ophthalmic artery, a branch of the internal carotid artery, supplies the eyeball.
It runs into the the orbit through the optic canal alongside the optic nerve,
and gives off the central artery of the retina and the ciliary arteries to supply the eyeball itself.

The ophthalmic artery also supplies other structures inside the orbit, such as the eye muscles and the lacrimal gland, and also some positioned nearby, like air sinuses and the meninges.

Ophthalmic artery

Internal carotid artery

Arterial supply to the eye seen from above.

The ophthalmic veins drain blood from the eyeball into the cavernous sinus.

Eye movements
The left eye, showing the muscles and nerves responsible for movement of the eye from the neutral position.

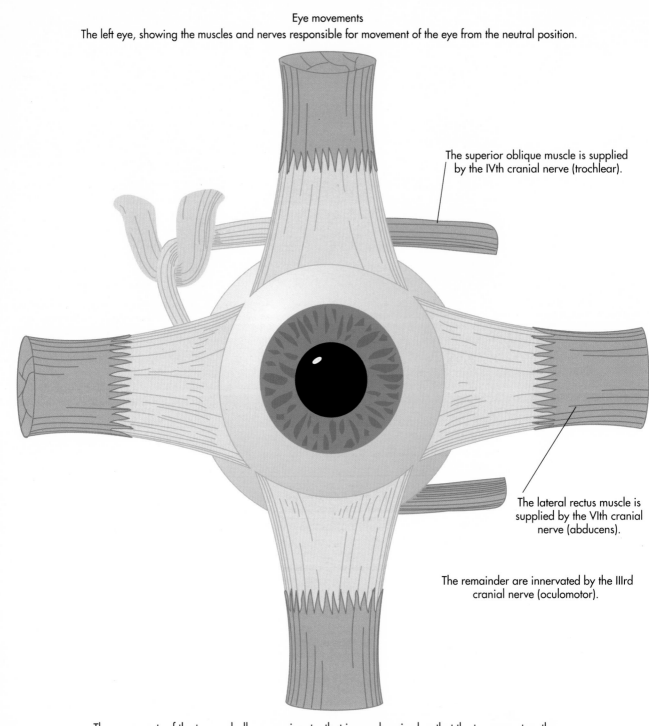

The superior oblique muscle is supplied by the IVth cranial nerve (trochlear).

The lateral rectus muscle is supplied by the VIth cranial nerve (abducens).

The remainder are innervated by the IIIrd cranial nerve (oculomotor).

The movements of the two eyeballs are conjugate, that is, synchronised so that the two move together.
The brain then fuses the two images it receives to give stereoscopic or three-dimensional vision.
This is a skill learnt in early childhood, which makes it possible to judge distances.

Conjugate eye movement is under both voluntary and reflex control.
The control centre is in the brain stem. It has links with:
— the cerebral cortex
— the medial longitudinal bundle, joining the nuclei of the nerves which move the eye muscles
(III, IV and VI cranial nerves)
— the vestibular nerves
— the cerebellum
— the neck muscles.

Clinically important movements are complex.
This is because the muscles act differently depending on the starting position of the eye;
in any case it is likely that in life, all the muscles act together to different degrees.
The topic is fully discussed in textbooks and journals of ophthalmology.

The eyelids, the lacrimal apparatus and tear production

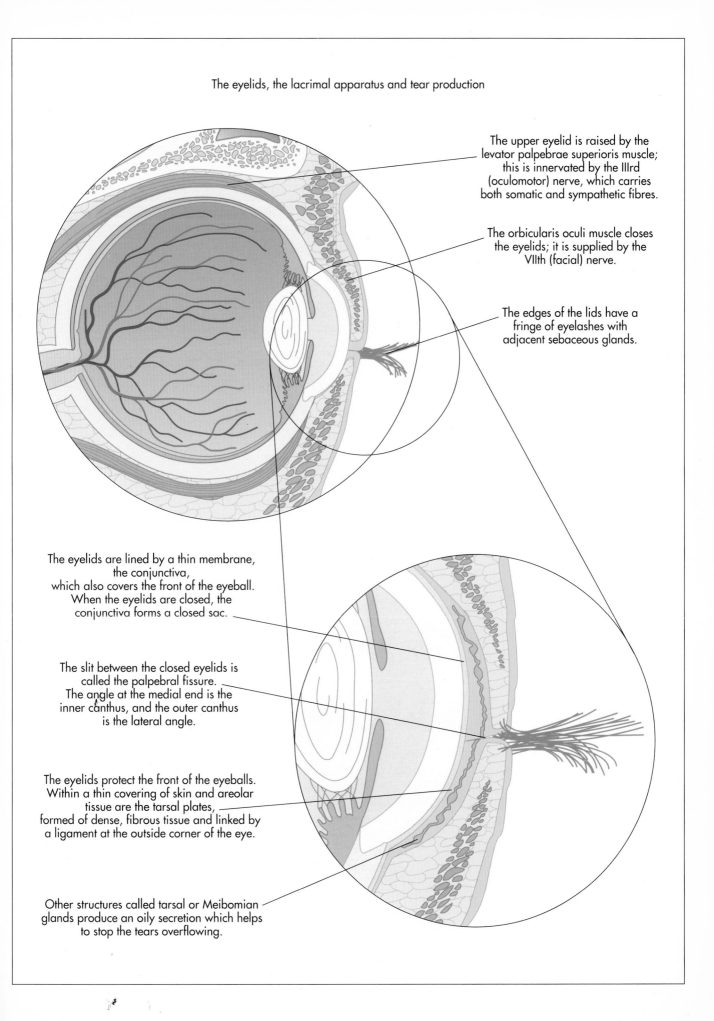

The upper eyelid is raised by the levator palpebrae superioris muscle; this is innervated by the IIIrd (oculomotor) nerve, which carries both somatic and sympathetic fibres.

The orbicularis oculi muscle closes the eyelids; it is supplied by the VIIth (facial) nerve.

The edges of the lids have a fringe of eyelashes with adjacent sebaceous glands.

The eyelids are lined by a thin membrane, the conjunctiva, which also covers the front of the eyeball. When the eyelids are closed, the conjunctiva forms a closed sac.

The slit between the closed eyelids is called the palpebral fissure. The angle at the medial end is the inner canthus, and the outer canthus is the lateral angle.

The eyelids protect the front of the eyeballs. Within a thin covering of skin and areolar tissue are the tarsal plates, formed of dense, fibrous tissue and linked by a ligament at the outside corner of the eye.

Other structures called tarsal or Meibomian glands produce an oily secretion which helps to stop the tears overflowing.

Tears are produced and circulated by the lacrimal apparatus.
The lacrimal gland secretes the tears down its tiny lacrimal ducts into the conjunctival sac.
When the orbicularis oculi muscle contracts during blinking, it milks the tears towards the inside corner of the eye.
Here they drain into the lacrimal canal, which opens at the lacrimal punctum.
They flow down the nasolacrimal duct and finally run into the nose below the inferior concha.

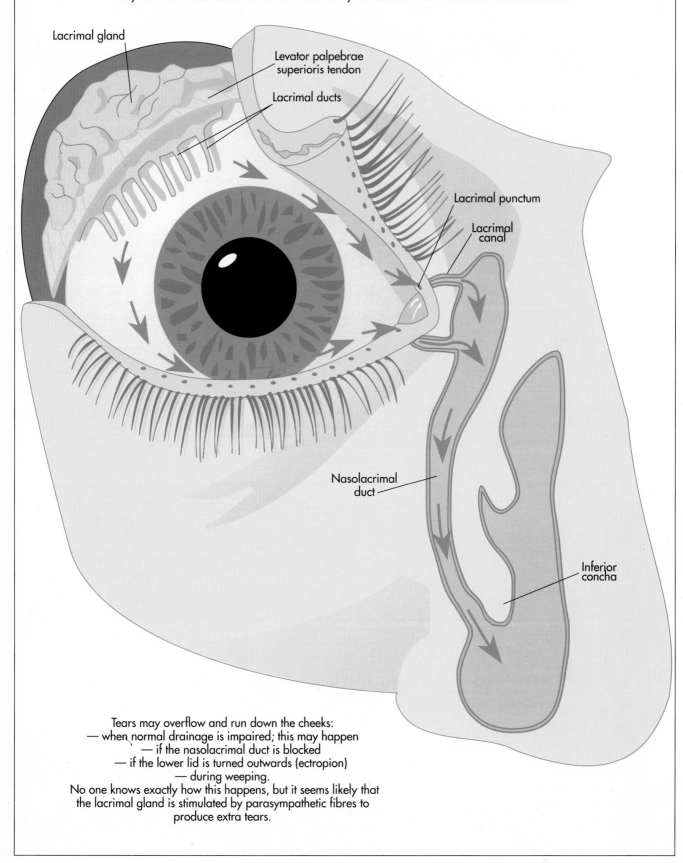

Lacrimal gland

Levator palpebrae
superioris tendon

Lacrimal ducts

Lacrimal punctum

Lacrimal
canal

Nasolacrimal
duct

Inferior
concha

Tears may overflow and run down the cheeks:
— when normal drainage is impaired; this may happen
— if the nasolacrimal duct is blocked
— if the lower lid is turned outwards (ectropion)
— during weeping.
No one knows exactly how this happens, but it seems likely that
the lacrimal gland is stimulated by parasympathetic fibres to
produce extra tears.

Visual fields and visual pathway

The visual field is the area over which someone can see. It is measured by perimetry.
This can be done clinically, by rough comparison with the examiner's normal eyes, or more accurately using machines.

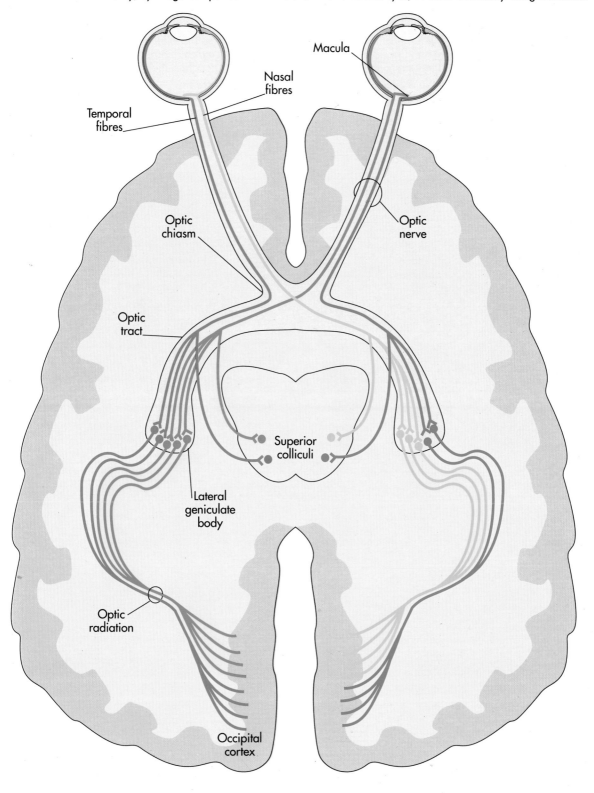

The visual pathway is the long, vulnerable tract that visual information
must travel between the eyes and the visual (occipital) cortex.

The retinal image is reversed from above to below and from left to right.
Retinal nerve fibres enter the optic nerve according to their position, and are
bundled together in the same relation to each other throughout their course.

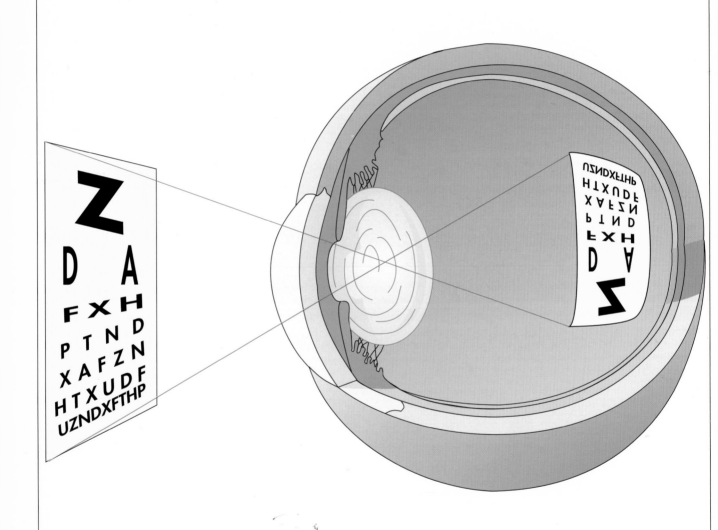

Disease and injuries of the visual pathway sometimes cause loss of part of the visual field.
Because the arrangement of the nerve fibres within the pathway is known, finding the size and
shape of a visual field defect shows where the damage has occurred.
This can help in the diagnosis of eye and brain disease.

The retina is a thin net of nervous tissue lying between the choroid and the hyaline membrane of the vitreous.
It develops as an outgrowth from the brain during embryonic life.
Postnatally it remains joined to the brain by the optic nerve at the optic disc or blind spot, which is insensitive to light.

The developing eye

Approximately 42 days

Approximately 28 days

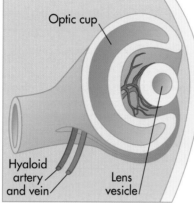

Approximately 32 days

Optic cup

Hyaloid
artery
and vein

Lens
vesicle

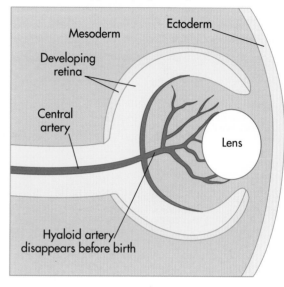

Mesoderm

Ectoderm

Developing
retina

Central
artery

Lens

Hyaloid artery
disappears before birth

Like all nervous tissue, the retina needs a good blood supply and is rapidly damaged if this is impaired.

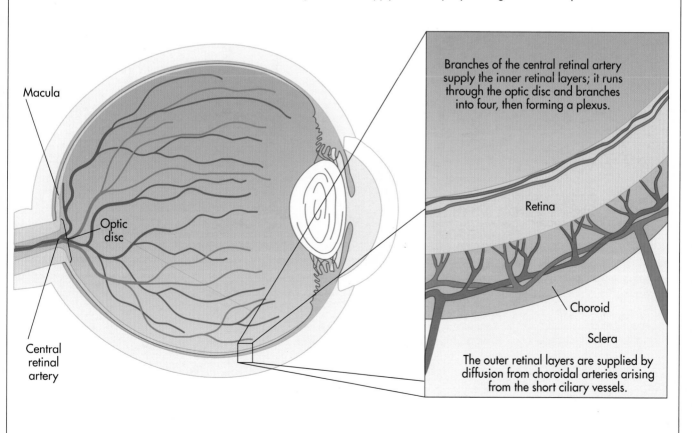

Macula

Optic
disc

Central
retinal
artery

Branches of the central retinal artery
supply the inner retinal layers; it runs
through the optic disc and branches
into four, then forming a plexus.

Retina

Choroid

Sclera

The outer retinal layers are supplied by
diffusion from choroidal arteries arising
from the short ciliary vessels.

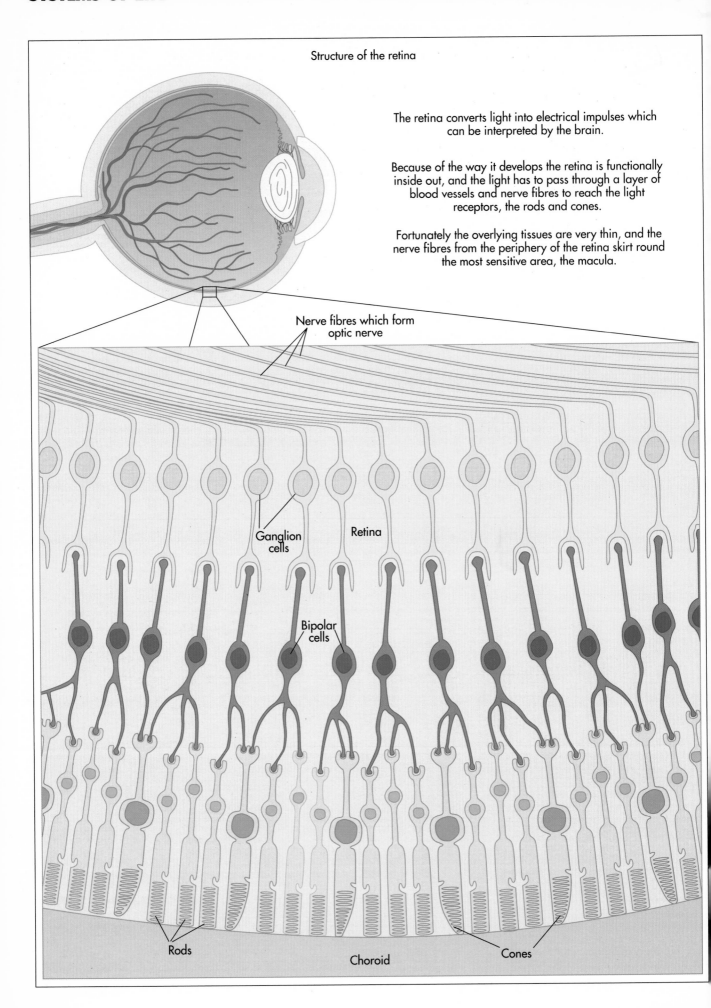

Structure of the retina

The retina converts light into electrical impulses which can be interpreted by the brain.

Because of the way it develops the retina is functionally inside out, and the light has to pass through a layer of blood vessels and nerve fibres to reach the light receptors, the rods and cones.

Fortunately the overlying tissues are very thin, and the nerve fibres from the periphery of the retina skirt round the most sensitive area, the macula.

Nerve fibres which form optic nerve

Ganglion cells

Retina

Bipolar cells

Rods

Cones

Choroid

Rods function in poor light; they 'see' in shades of grey (scotopic vision).
The rods are thickest round the edges of the retina, well away from the macula.
Someone trying to see an object in poor light (eg an astronomer looking at a faint star) will look beside it rather than directly at it.
This will bring its image onto the sensitive, rod-rich periphery of the retina.
Rods contain the pigment rhodopsin, bleached by light, releasing chemical energy.
This is converted to electrical energy, which stimulates the optic nerve, sending messages to the brain about what is seen.

Dark adaptation
People who spend some time in poorly lit surroundings gradually see them more clearly.
This happens because
— rhodopsin accumulates
— the pupil dilates, letting more light into the eye
— light receptors are stimulated over a wider and wider area (spatial summation)
— light input to individual receptors adds up as time passes (temporal summation).

Cones function in daylight, 'seeing' in colour (photopic vision).
The cones are concentrated at the macula, about 3mm to the temporal side of the optic disc. This area is therefore specialised to see in colour and fine detail.
There are three types of cones, each with a different photosensitive pigment.
Each of these absorbs light from a particular wavelength of the spectrum.
One set is for blue-violet light, another for green light and a third for yellow-red.

Colour vision depends on
— how much each group of receptors is stimulated
— how the resulting nerve impulses are perceived in the brain.

Equal stimulation of all receptors makes the brain perceive white.
Black absorbs all light, so none is reflected from a black object to stimulate the cones. The brain perceives the 'non-colour', black.

Aqueous and vitreous humour
Aqueous humour carries oxygen and nutrients to and waste products away from the cornea and lens.
Blood is the transport medium of the rest of the body,
but cannot be used here as the red vessels would get in the way of the light pathway and obscure vision.
Aqueous is produced in the ciliary processes by ultrafiltration:
the blood is 'strained', and cells and large molecules stay behind in the circulation.
The remaining fluid which is secreted into the posterior chamber is perfectly clear, so light can shine through it.
From the ciliary processes the fluid flows behind the iris and through the pupil into the anterior chamber.
Here it is reabsorbed into the ocular veins via the canal of Schlemm.

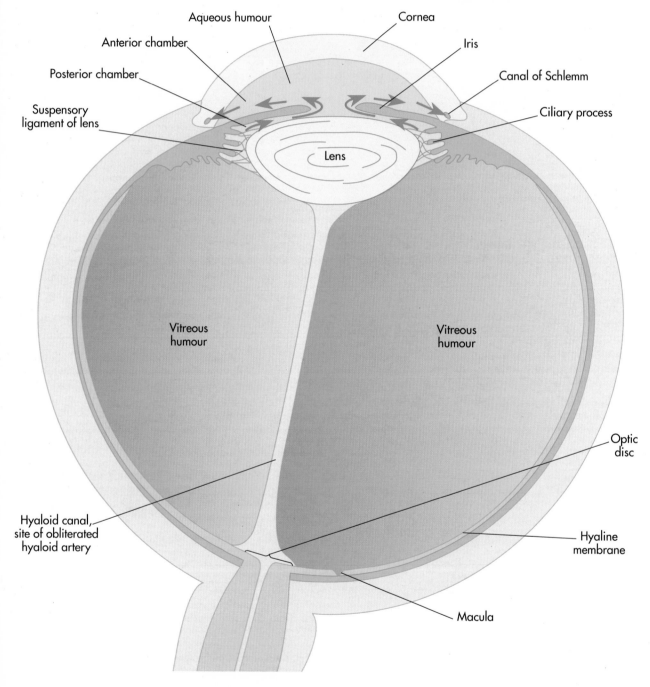

The vitreous humour, also called the vitreous body, occupies the rest of the eyeball.
It consists of a gel which contains fibres; these thicken peripherally to form a hyaline membrane.
The lens fits into a hollow at the front of the vitreous.
Around it the fibres of the vitreous condense like the spokes of a wheel to form the suspensory ligament of the lens.
This runs between the ciliary processes and the lens capsule, and allows the lens to change shape during accomodation.
The vitreous cannot contain blood vessels without impairing its transparency;
it therefore gets its nourishment from the retinal and ciliary vessels around it.

Refraction, the lens and accommodation

Refraction is the process by which light rays are bent
as they pass from one substance to another.
Because of it, the eye can bring rays of light from a
large field to focus on the small area of the retina.

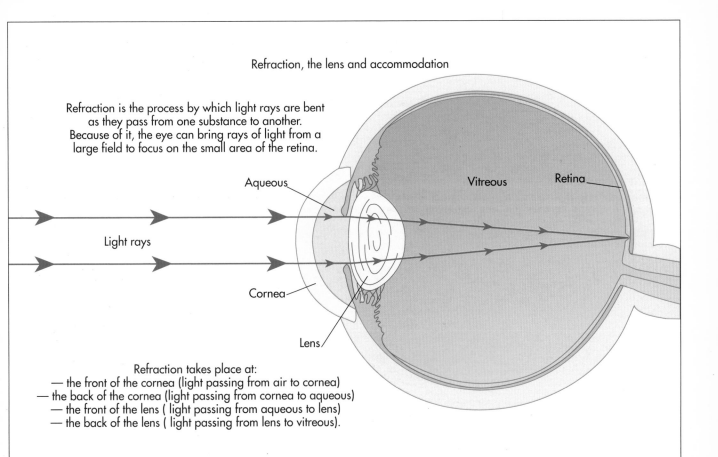

Refraction takes place at:
— the front of the cornea (light passing from air to cornea)
— the back of the cornea (light passing from cornea to aqueous)
— the front of the lens (light passing from aqueous to lens)
— the back of the lens (light passing from lens to vitreous).

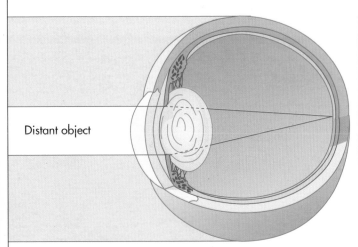

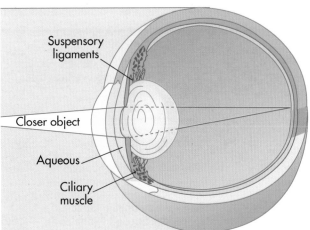

Because the lens can change its shape, it can
alter the amount it bends light rays.
This enables objects at different distances from
the eye to be seen clearly,
as the light rays reflected from them can be
brought to a sharp focus on the retina.

When the ciliary muscle contracts into a tighter circle, the
tension on the suspensory ligament is released.
As the lens is elastic, it then springs back into a fatter shape.

At the same time
— the iris constricts the pupil, so that light only falls on the
most curved part of the lens
— the medial recti contract to converge the visual axes of
the two eyes.
(The ciliary muscle, the muscle of the iris and the medial
recti are all supplied by the oculomotor (IIIrd) nerve).

This three-part process is called accommodation.
For distant vision, the ciliary muscle relaxes into a looser circle,
and the suspensory ligament pulls the lens into a thinner shape.

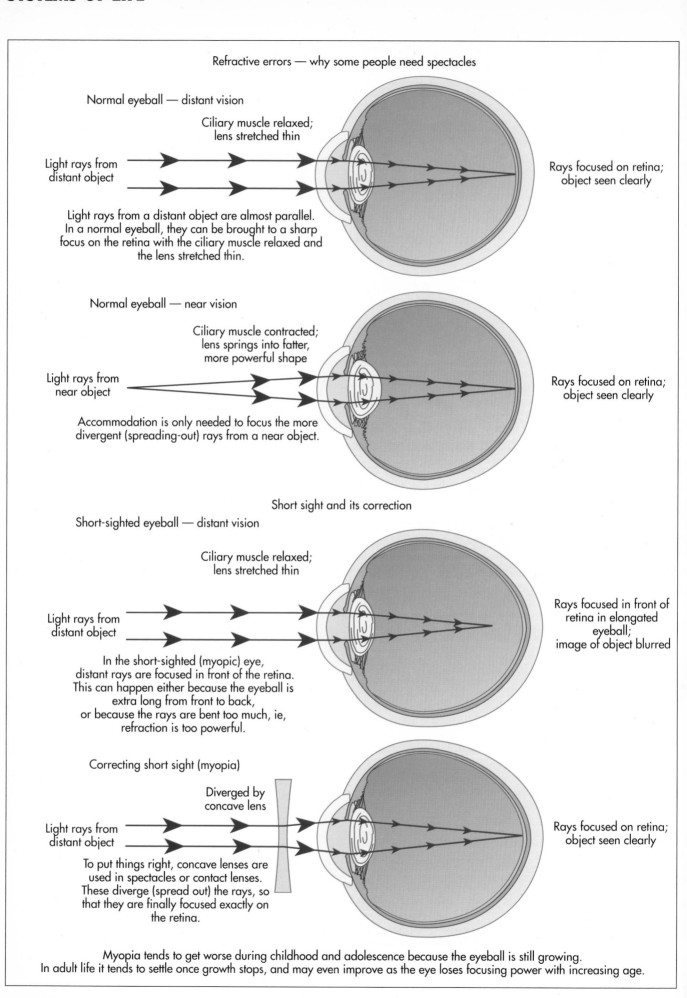

Refractive errors — why some people need spectacles

Normal eyeball — distant vision

Ciliary muscle relaxed;
lens stretched thin

Light rays from
distant object

Rays focused on retina;
object seen clearly

Light rays from a distant object are almost parallel.
In a normal eyeball, they can be brought to a sharp
focus on the retina with the ciliary muscle relaxed and
the lens stretched thin.

Normal eyeball — near vision

Ciliary muscle contracted;
lens springs into fatter,
more powerful shape

Light rays from
near object

Rays focused on retina;
object seen clearly

Accommodation is only needed to focus the more
divergent (spreading-out) rays from a near object.

Short sight and its correction

Short-sighted eyeball — distant vision

Ciliary muscle relaxed;
lens stretched thin

Light rays from
distant object

Rays focused in front of
retina in elongated
eyeball;
image of object blurred

In the short-sighted (myopic) eye,
distant rays are focused in front of the retina.
This can happen either because the eyeball is
extra long from front to back,
or because the rays are bent too much, ie,
refraction is too powerful.

Correcting short sight (myopia)

Diverged by
concave lens

Light rays from
distant object

Rays focused on retina;
object seen clearly

To put things right, concave lenses are
used in spectacles or contact lenses.
These diverge (spread out) the rays, so
that they are finally focused exactly on
the retina.

Myopia tends to get worse during childhood and adolescence because the eyeball is still growing.
In adult life it tends to settle once growth stops, and may even improve as the eye loses focusing power with increasing age.

Long sight (hypermetropia) and its correction

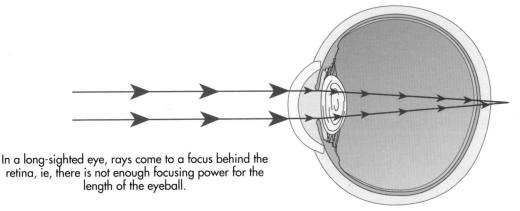

Rays of light focused behind retina; image of object blurred

In a long-sighted eye, rays come to a focus behind the retina, ie, there is not enough focusing power for the length of the eyeball.

Correcting long sight

Converged by convex lens

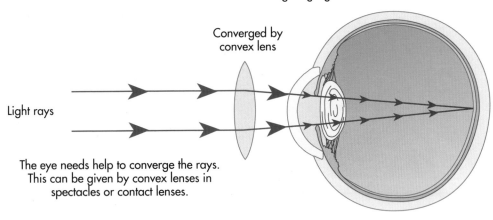

Light rays

Rays focused on retina; object seen clearly

The eye needs help to converge the rays. This can be given by convex lenses in spectacles or contact lenses.

Presbyopia ('old vision')

Long-sighted eyeball using accommodation for distant vision

Ciliary muscle contracted; lens more powerful

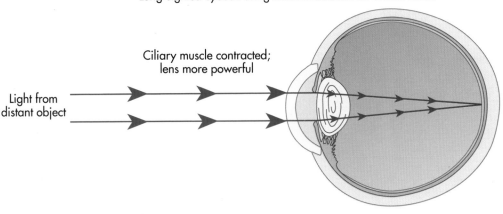

Light from distant object

Rays focused on retina; object seen clearly

A long-sighted young person can compensate to some extent by extra accommodation, ie, forming the lens into its fatter, more powerful shape even for distant objects. However, this then leaves little extra refractive power for viewing near objects, as the ciliary muscle cannot contract much further and the lens cannot become much fatter.

Ageing changes in the lens (presbyopia) affect both long-sighted and short-sighted people. As the years pass, the lens becomes stiffer and less elastic, so it cannot vary its shape so much during accommodation. Seeing near objects clearly becomes more difficult, and glasses are needed for close work such as reading. These contain convex lenses to give added power to the ageing lens. People who were long-sighted in early life and have little spare focusing capacity need reading glasses earlier than short-sighted people, who have some focusing power to spare.

Perception — the psychology of sight

The brain tries to make sense of its surroundings.
Its interpretation of the images it receives from the eyes is influenced by what it has learnt in the past.

It has difficulty with impossible objects, like these.

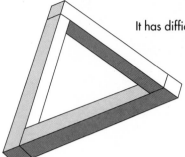

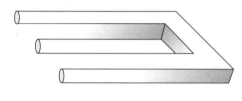

Familiar objects can be recognised even when their images are differently shaped

Edge on

Flat — Full face

Half-face forming an ellipse

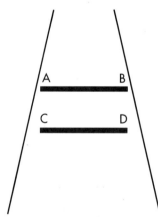

In the figure, lines AB and CD are the same length,
but the brain 'sees' AB as longer because it has learnt about perspective.
If the horizontal lines were sleepers on a railway track receding into the distance, their
image would diminish in length the further away they were from the eye.
The brain knows that sleepers are the same length,
despite the fact that they appear to shorten with distance,
so when AB does not appear shorter than CD,
the brain assumes that it is in fact longer.
Sleepers that did not appear to diminish in size
would in fact be longer than their nearer counterparts.

SHADOW

Again, the brain can be deceived into 'seeing' things that are not there.
If presented with dark shapes as possible shadows, it can imagine the objects that cast them.

THE EAR AND HEARING

The function of the ear is to process information reaching it as sound into a form which can be analysed by the brain.
The ear is divided into three parts:
the outer or external ear,
the middle ear or tympanic cavity
and the inner ear or labyrinth.

The outer ear collects sound, the middle ear transmits and
amplifies sound and the inner ear interprets sound.

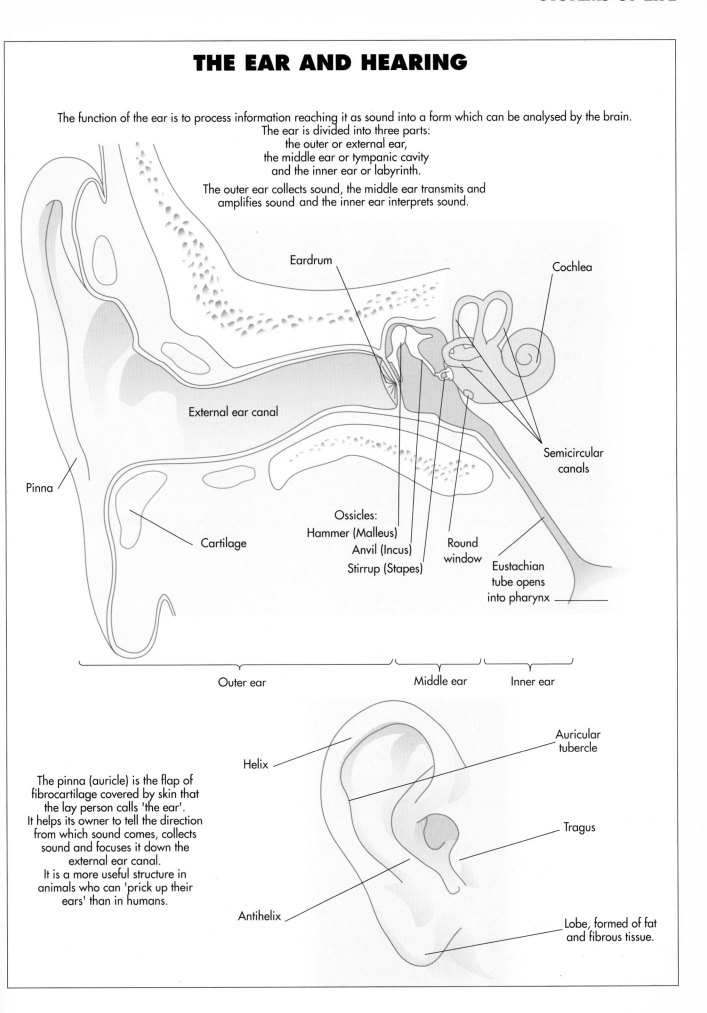

Eardrum

Cochlea

External ear canal

Pinna

Cartilage

Ossicles:
Hammer (Malleus)
Anvil (Incus)
Stirrup (Stapes)

Round
window

Semicircular
canals

Eustachian
tube opens
into pharynx

Outer ear

Middle ear

Inner ear

Helix

Auricular
tubercle

Tragus

Antihelix

Lobe, formed of fat
and fibrous tissue.

The pinna (auricle) is the flap of
fibrocartilage covered by skin that
the lay person calls 'the ear'.
It helps its owner to tell the direction
from which sound comes, collects
sound and focuses it down the
external ear canal.
It is a more useful structure in
animals who can 'prick up their
ears' than in humans.

The outer or external ear

The outer ear consists of the pinna (auricle) and the external ear canal.
This ends at the eardrum (tympanic membrane), which divides the outer from the middle ear.

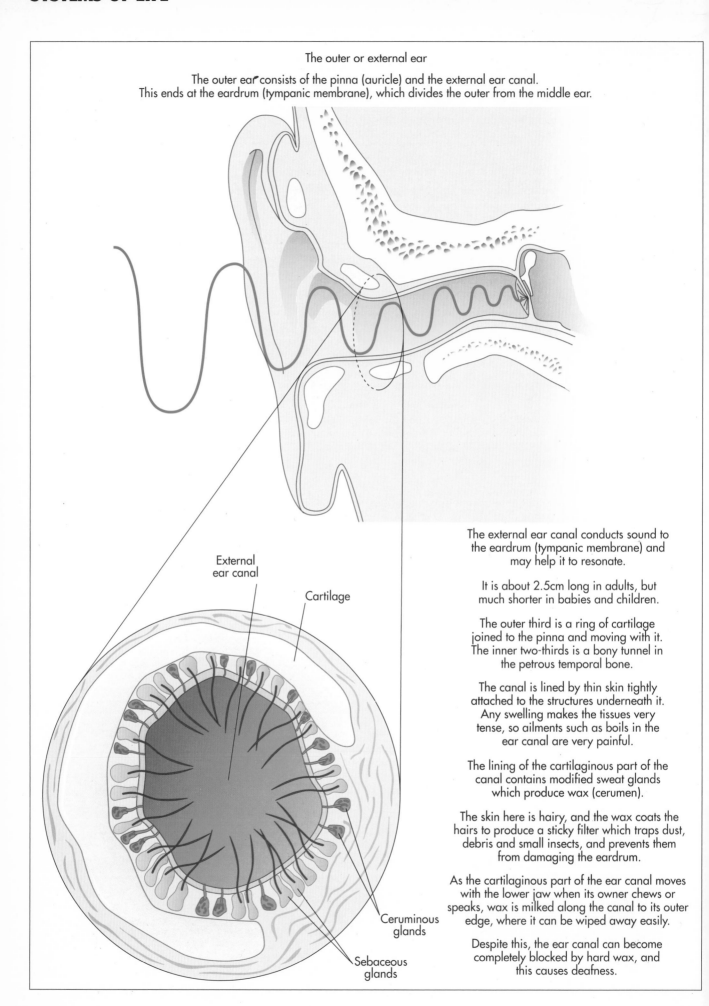

External
ear canal

Cartilage

Ceruminous
glands

Sebaceous
glands

The external ear canal conducts sound to the eardrum (tympanic membrane) and may help it to resonate.

It is about 2.5cm long in adults, but much shorter in babies and children.

The outer third is a ring of cartilage joined to the pinna and moving with it. The inner two-thirds is a bony tunnel in the petrous temporal bone.

The canal is lined by thin skin tightly attached to the structures underneath it. Any swelling makes the tissues very tense, so ailments such as boils in the ear canal are very painful.

The lining of the cartilaginous part of the canal contains modified sweat glands which produce wax (cerumen).

The skin here is hairy, and the wax coats the hairs to produce a sticky filter which traps dust, debris and small insects, and prevents them from damaging the eardrum.

As the cartilaginous part of the ear canal moves with the lower jaw when its owner chews or speaks, wax is milked along the canal to its outer edge, where it can be wiped away easily.

Despite this, the ear canal can become completely blocked by hard wax, and this causes deafness.

The eardrum (tympanic membrane) is the boundary between the outer and middle ear.

It has three layers:
— outer epithelium continuous with the skin lining the external ear canal
— a middle layer of fibres
— an inner layer of mucous membrane.

Pulling back the pinna straightens the cartilaginous part of the ear canal and gives the best view of the eardrum through an auriscope.

It is set at an angle in the canal and held within it by an incomplete ring of fibrocartilage. The upper part of the membrane is thin and lax (pars flaccida), while the lower part is stretched and thick (pars tensa). The handle of the malleus is attached to the inner side of the membrane and pulls it inwards, so that the outer surface is concave. The membrane is least vascular below and posteriorly, so this is the best place to incise it.

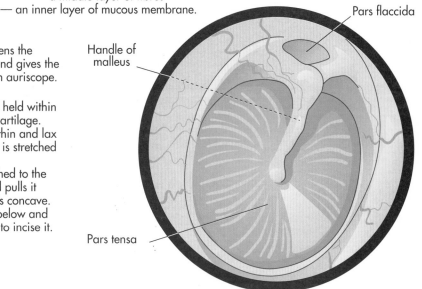

Pars flaccida

Handle of malleus

Pars tensa

Radial fibres   Circular fibres

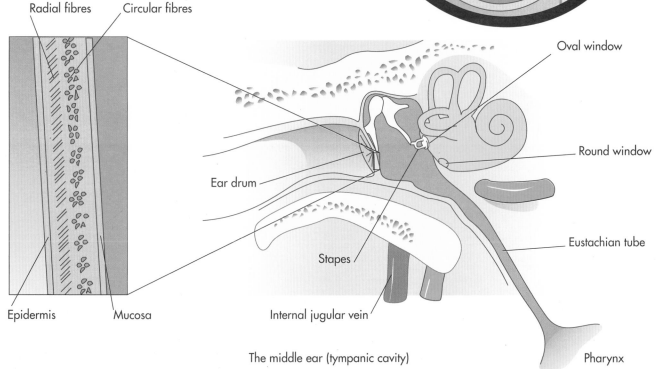

Oval window

Round window

Ear drum

Eustachian tube

Stapes

Epidermis   Mucosa   Internal jugular vein

Pharynx

The middle ear (tympanic cavity)

This is an air-filled cleft in the temporal bone which is lined by mucous membrane.

The eardrum forms its lateral wall.
Above, a thin plate of bone separates the cavity from the inside of the skull.
Infection can easily spread to the brain by this route, especially in young children before the sutures close.

Below the thin bony floor of the middle ear run the internal jugular vein and the glossopharyngeal nerve.

The auditory tube (pharyngotympanic or Eustachian tube) runs between the tympanic cavity and the nasal part of the pharynx.
The tube is normally closed, but muscles open it when its owner swallows or yawns.
Opening the tube equalises the pressure on either side of the eardrum during changes of altitude, for instance during a flight in an aircraft.

The medial wall of the tympanic cavity divides it from the inner ear.
The facial nerve runs through a canal in the bone and the stapes sits in the oval window (fenestra vestibuli) with the round window (fenestra cochleae) below it.

A gap in the posterior wall of the middle ear cavity, the aditus, leads into the mastoid antrum which opens into the other mastoid air cells in the petrous temporal bone.

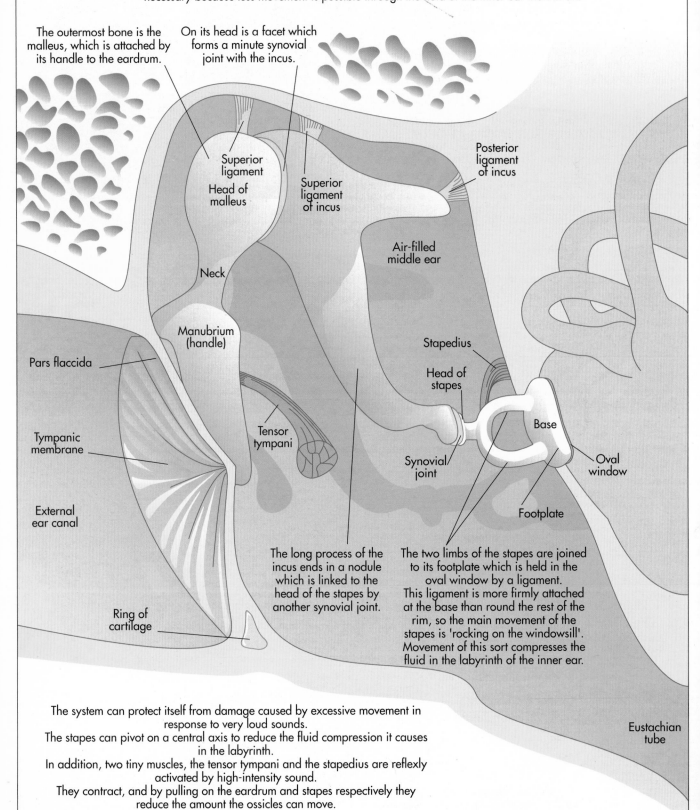

The ossicles of the middle ear
These were named by imaginative anatomists according to their shape:
the malleus (hammer),
incus (anvil),
and stapes (stirrup).
They form a chain across the middle ear, transmitting the vibrations of the eardrum to the hearing organ of the inner ear.
In doing so, they magnify the movement 25-fold
— necessary because less movement is possible through the fluid of the inner ear than in air.

The outermost bone is the malleus, which is attached by its handle to the eardrum.

On its head is a facet which forms a minute synovial joint with the incus.

Superior ligament

Head of malleus

Superior ligament of incus

Posterior ligament of incus

Air-filled middle ear

Neck

Manubrium (handle)

Stapedius

Head of stapes

Base

Pars flaccida

Tympanic membrane

Tensor tympani

Synovial joint

Oval window

External ear canal

Footplate

Ring of cartilage

The long process of the incus ends in a nodule which is linked to the head of the stapes by another synovial joint.

The two limbs of the stapes are joined to its footplate which is held in the oval window by a ligament. This ligament is more firmly attached at the base than round the rest of the rim, so the main movement of the stapes is 'rocking on the windowsill'. Movement of this sort compresses the fluid in the labyrinth of the inner ear.

Eustachian tube

The system can protect itself from damage caused by excessive movement in response to very loud sounds.
The stapes can pivot on a central axis to reduce the fluid compression it causes in the labyrinth.
In addition, two tiny muscles, the tensor tympani and the stapedius are reflexly activated by high-intensity sound.
They contract, and by pulling on the eardrum and stapes respectively they reduce the amount the ossicles can move.

The inner ear or labyrinth
The inner ear has two functions:
hearing and the control of balance.
It consists of the bony labyrinth, a series of tunnels in the petrous temporal bone, connected to a cave, the vestibule.

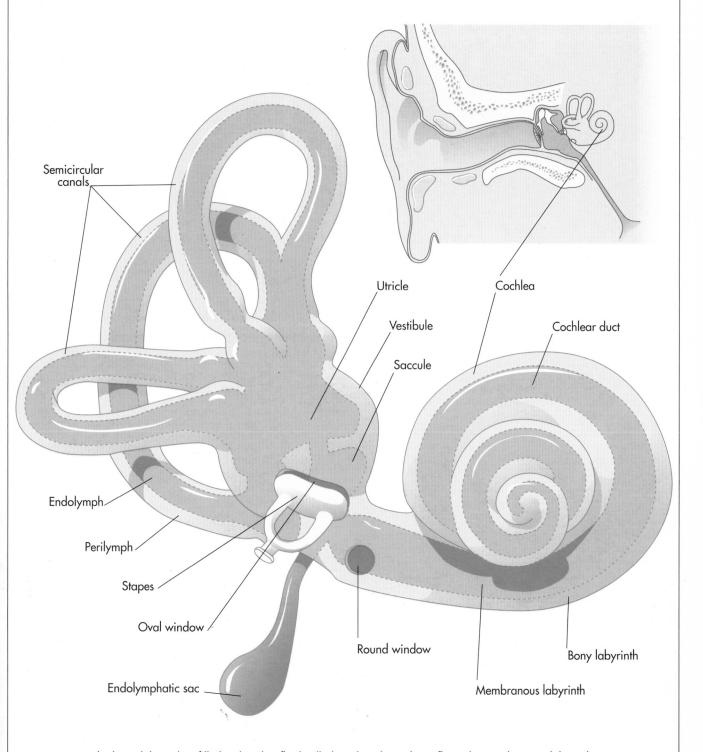

Semicircular canals

Utricle

Cochlea

Vestibule

Cochlear duct

Saccule

Endolymph

Perilymph

Stapes

Oval window

Round window

Bony labyrinth

Endolymphatic sac

Membranous labyrinth

The bony labyrinth is filled with a thin fluid called perilymph, and in it floats the membranous labyrinth.
This comprises the three semicircular canals, the utricle and saccule and the cochlear duct.
The membranous labyrinth contains a thick, viscous fluid called endolymph.

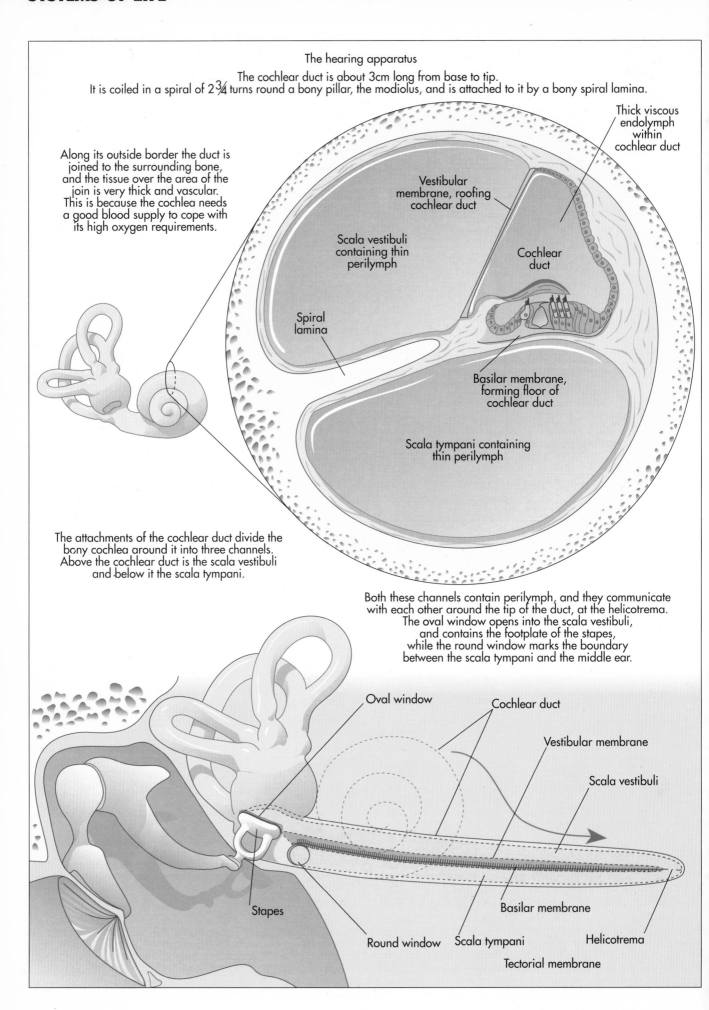

The hearing apparatus
The cochlear duct is about 3cm long from base to tip.
It is coiled in a spiral of 2¾ turns round a bony pillar, the modiolus, and is attached to it by a bony spiral lamina.

Thick viscous endolymph within cochlear duct

Vestibular membrane, roofing cochlear duct

Along its outside border the duct is joined to the surrounding bone, and the tissue over the area of the join is very thick and vascular. This is because the cochlea needs a good blood supply to cope with its high oxygen requirements.

Scala vestibuli containing thin perilymph

Cochlear duct

Spiral lamina

Basilar membrane, forming floor of cochlear duct

Scala tympani containing thin perilymph

The attachments of the cochlear duct divide the bony cochlea around it into three channels. Above the cochlear duct is the scala vestibuli and below it the scala tympani.

Both these channels contain perilymph, and they communicate with each other around the tip of the duct, at the helicotrema. The oval window opens into the scala vestibuli, and contains the footplate of the stapes, while the round window marks the boundary between the scala tympani and the middle ear.

Oval window

Cochlear duct

Vestibular membrane

Scala vestibuli

Stapes

Basilar membrane

Round window   Scala tympani   Helicotrema

Tectorial membrane

How the hearing apparatus works

When the stapes rocks back and forth in the oval window,
it creates pressure waves in the perilymph in the scala vestibuli.
This is transmitted to the endolymph of the cochlear duct
and causes a wave of movement in the basilar membrane.
The site at which the membrane is bent most
depends on the wavelength of the original sound.
High-frequency sounds produce most movement near the oval window,
while low frequencies have most effect near the helicotrema.

On the basilar membrane lies the organ of Corti.
Because of its special structure, it can translate
the wave motion into nerve impulses.

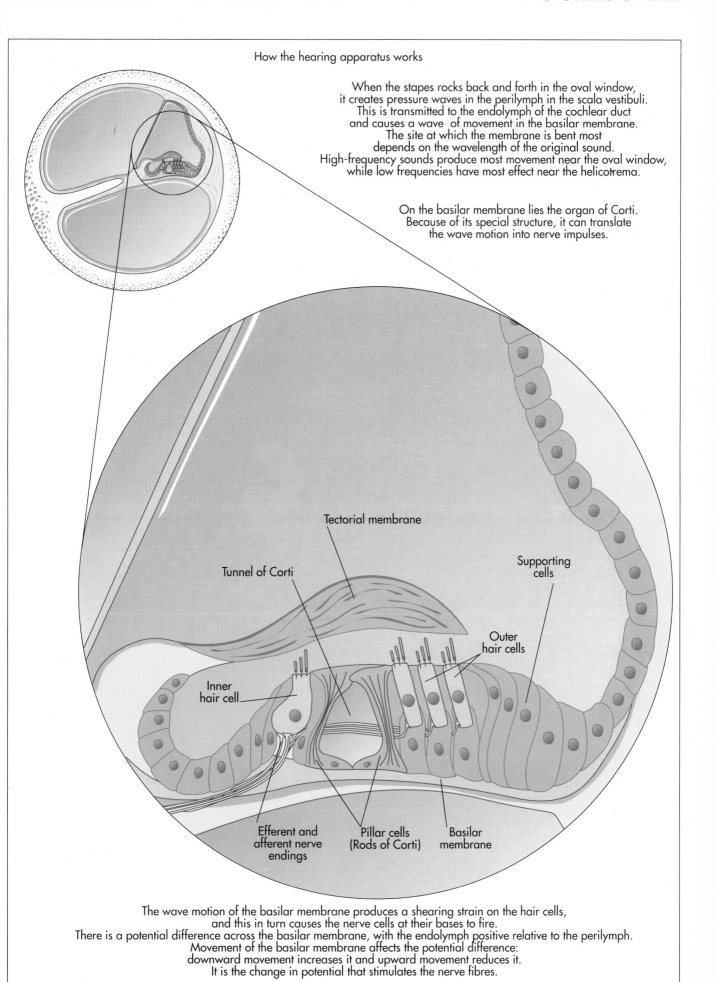

Tectorial membrane

Tunnel of Corti

Supporting cells

Outer hair cells

Inner hair cell

Efferent and afferent nerve endings

Pillar cells (Rods of Corti)

Basilar membrane

The wave motion of the basilar membrane produces a shearing strain on the hair cells,
and this in turn causes the nerve cells at their bases to fire.
There is a potential difference across the basilar membrane, with the endolymph positive relative to the perilymph.
Movement of the basilar membrane affects the potential difference:
downward movement increases it and upward movement reduces it.
It is the change in potential that stimulates the nerve fibres.

The hearing pathway

Sound information from the ear is relayed to the brain, where it can be
analysed for meaning and compared with stored memories.

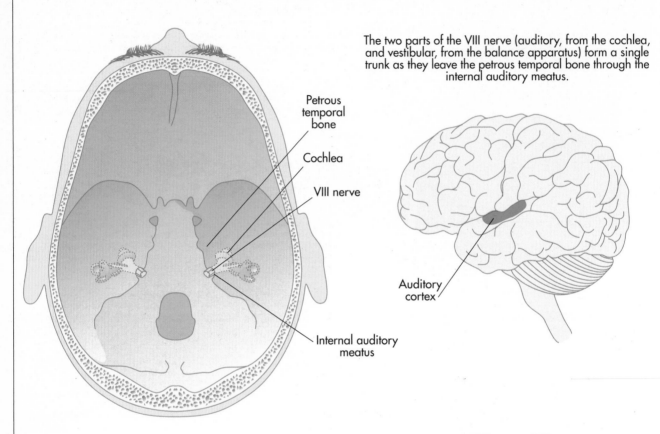

The two parts of the VIII nerve (auditory, from the cochlea,
and vestibular, from the balance apparatus) form a single
trunk as they leave the petrous temporal bone through the
internal auditory meatus.

Petrous
temporal
bone

Cochlea

VIII nerve

Auditory
cortex

Internal auditory
meatus

1. The VIII nerve runs beside the VII nerve through the
cerebellopontine angle (angle between the cerebellum
and the pons), and enters the brain stem at the lower
border of the pons.

2. Fibres from the cochlea then run to the cochlear
(auditory) nuclei below the floor of the 4th ventricle.

3. They relay on as the lateral lemnisci, which run up
the brain stem to the inferior colliculi and on to the
medial geniculate bodies, where they synapse.

4. From here, fibres pass to the auditory
cortex in the temporal lobe, where sound
information is analysed.

Information from each ear projects to both sides of the cortex.
This means that information from the right ear reaches both right
and left temporal lobes, and vice versa.
Because of this, deafness is hardly ever due to cortical disease.

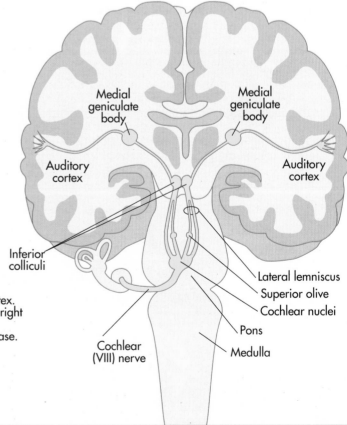

Medial
geniculate
body

Medial
geniculate
body

Auditory
cortex

Auditory
cortex

Inferior
colliculi

Lateral lemniscus

Superior olive

Cochlear nuclei

Pons

Cochlear
(VIII) nerve

Medulla

How sound travels through the ear — summary

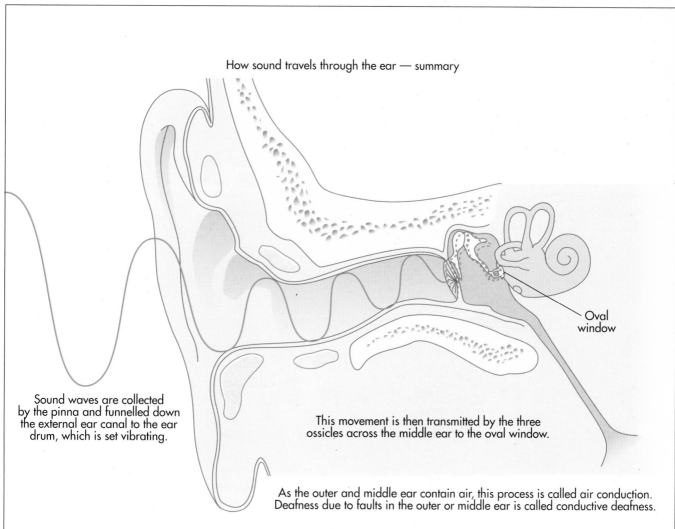

Oval
window

Sound waves are collected
by the pinna and funnelled down
the external ear canal to the ear
drum, which is set vibrating.

This movement is then transmitted by the three
ossicles across the middle ear to the oval window.

As the outer and middle ear contain air, this process is called air conduction.
Deafness due to faults in the outer or middle ear is called conductive deafness.

The oval window forms the boundary between the middle and inner ear.
The inner ear is filled with fluid, and the arrangement of the middle ear ossicles helps to
avoid too much loss of energy as the sound waves pass from one medium to another.

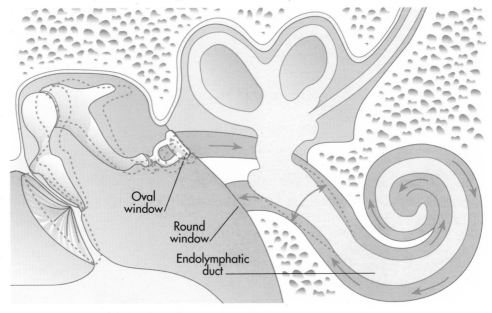

Oval
window

Round
window

Endolymphatic
duct

Movement of the oval window sets up pressure waves in the inner ear perilymph,
distorting the endolymphatic duct in the shape of a wave.
The point at which the duct is most distorted corresponds to the wavelength of the original sound.
At this point a shearing strain is produced across the hair cells of the basilar membrane,
and the bending of their cilia causes the auditory nerve cells to fire.

Tuning fork tests

Sound waves normally reach the inner ear through the air in the outer and middle ear (air conduction).
However, sound produces some vibration in the skull itself, and this reaches the inner ear by bone conduction.
Identifying differences between air and bone conduction can help to tell conductive and perceptive deafness apart.

In Rinne's test a vibrating tuning fork is held close to the patient's ear,
so that the sound reaches the inner ear by air conduction (1).

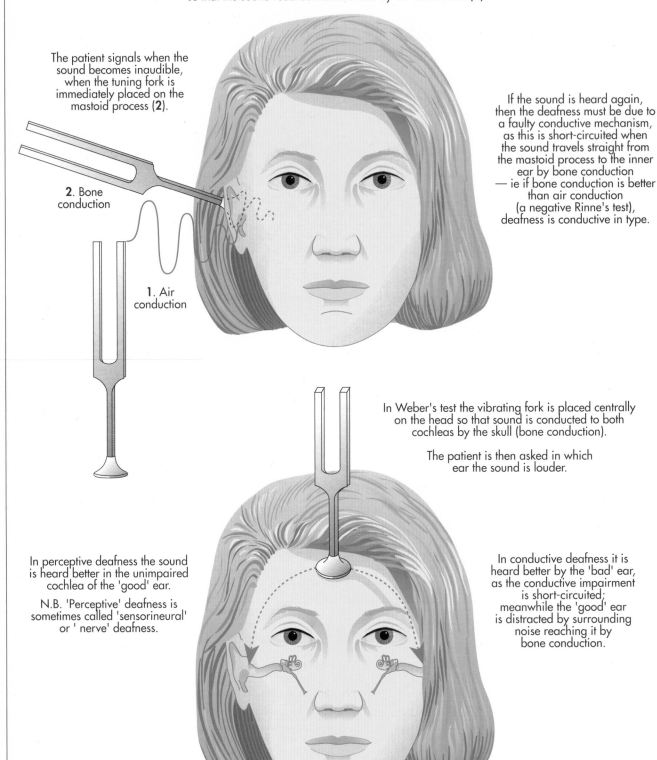

The patient signals when the
sound becomes inaudible,
when the tuning fork is
immediately placed on the
mastoid process (2).

2. Bone
conduction

1. Air
conduction

If the sound is heard again,
then the deafness must be due to
a faulty conductive mechanism,
as this is short-circuited when
the sound travels straight from
the mastoid process to the inner
ear by bone conduction
— ie if bone conduction is better
than air conduction
(a negative Rinne's test),
deafness is conductive in type.

In Weber's test the vibrating fork is placed centrally
on the head so that sound is conducted to both
cochleas by the skull (bone conduction).

The patient is then asked in which
ear the sound is louder.

In perceptive deafness the sound
is heard better in the unimpaired
cochlea of the 'good' ear.

N.B. 'Perceptive' deafness is
sometimes called 'sensorineural'
or ' nerve' deafness.

In conductive deafness it is
heard better by the 'bad' ear,
as the conductive impairment
is short-circuited;
meanwhile the 'good' ear
is distracted by surrounding
noise reaching it by
bone conduction.

A healthy person with no hearing impairment hears the sound equally well in both ears.

The inner ear and balance

The vestibular apparatus feeds information about position and movement of the head in space
into the brain via the vestibular division of the VIII nerve.

The parts of the bony labyrinth concerned with balance are the
semicircular canals and vestibule, which contain perilymph.

The membranous labyrinth floats within; this consists of three membranous semicircular canals,
the utricle and saccule, all filled with endolymph.

The three semicircular canals lie in planes at right angles to each other.
Each has an expanded portion at one junction with the utricle: this is the ampulla.

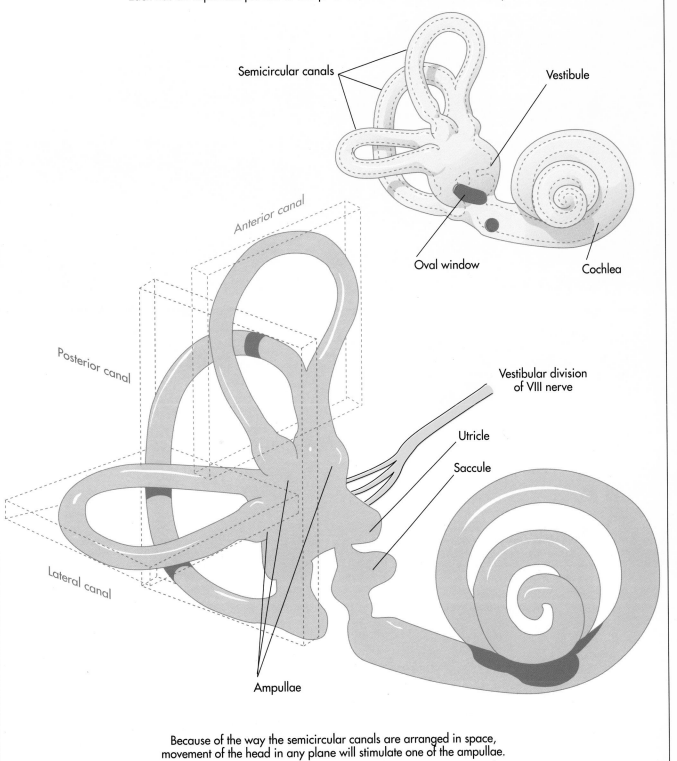

Semicircular canals

Vestibule

Oval window

Cochlea

Anterior canal

Posterior canal

Lateral canal

Vestibular division
of VIII nerve

Utricle

Saccule

Ampullae

Because of the way the semicircular canals are arranged in space,
movement of the head in any plane will stimulate one of the ampullae.

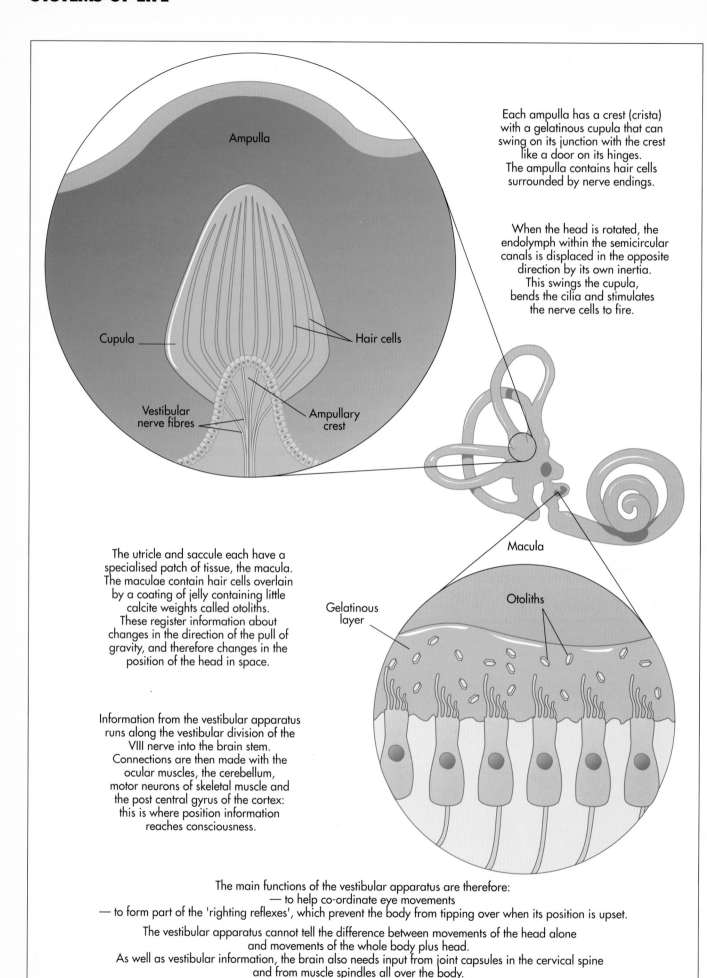

Ampulla

Each ampulla has a crest (crista) with a gelatinous cupula that can swing on its junction with the crest like a door on its hinges. The ampulla contains hair cells surrounded by nerve endings.

When the head is rotated, the endolymph within the semicircular canals is displaced in the opposite direction by its own inertia. This swings the cupula, bends the cilia and stimulates the nerve cells to fire.

Hair cells

Cupula

Vestibular nerve fibres

Ampullary crest

The utricle and saccule each have a specialised patch of tissue, the macula. The maculae contain hair cells overlain by a coating of jelly containing little calcite weights called otoliths. These register information about changes in the direction of the pull of gravity, and therefore changes in the position of the head in space.

Macula

Otoliths

Gelatinous layer

Information from the vestibular apparatus runs along the vestibular division of the VIII nerve into the brain stem. Connections are then made with the ocular muscles, the cerebellum, motor neurons of skeletal muscle and the post central gyrus of the cortex: this is where position information reaches consciousness.

The main functions of the vestibular apparatus are therefore:
— to help co-ordinate eye movements
— to form part of the 'righting reflexes', which prevent the body from tipping over when its position is upset.

The vestibular apparatus cannot tell the difference between movements of the head alone and movements of the whole body plus head.
As well as vestibular information, the brain also needs input from joint capsules in the cervical spine and from muscle spindles all over the body.

SMELL

The sense of smell is vital to many animals.
It helps them to hunt for food, to detect and escape from predators and to recognise family or pack members.
In humans smell is less important, but it is helpful in:
— digestion: saliva and gastric juice are secreted in response to food smells;
— detection of some dangers, such as smoke, gas, rotten food and infection hazards such as faeces and carrion;
— the sense of taste;
— possibly, as an influence on emotional states

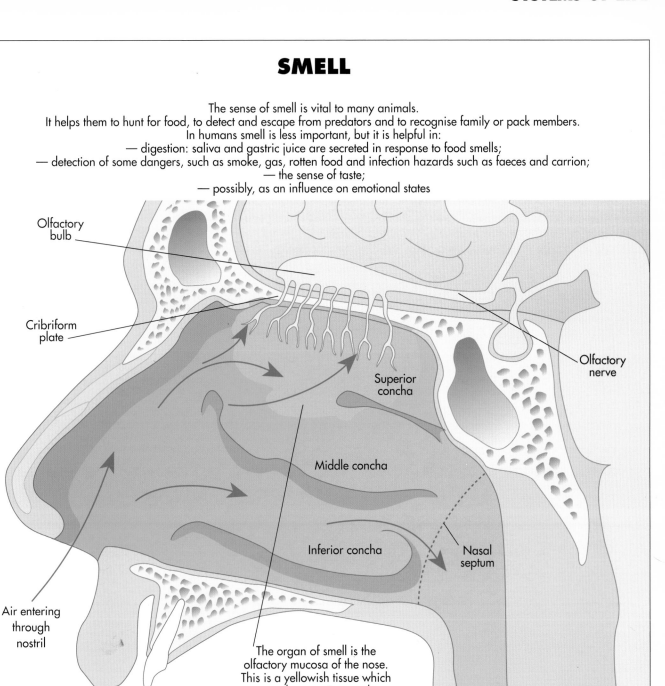

Olfactory bulb

Cribriform plate

Olfactory nerve

Superior concha

Middle concha

Inferior concha

Nasal septum

Air entering through nostril

The organ of smell is the olfactory mucosa of the nose. This is a yellowish tissue which covers the superior concha, the roof of the nasal cavity and the upper part of the nasal septum.

Inhaled air passes below the olfactory mucosa A deep sniff brings more air into contact with the receptor cells, and is therefore a good way of capturing scent.

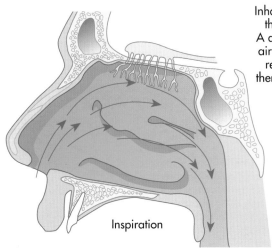

Inspiration

Expiration

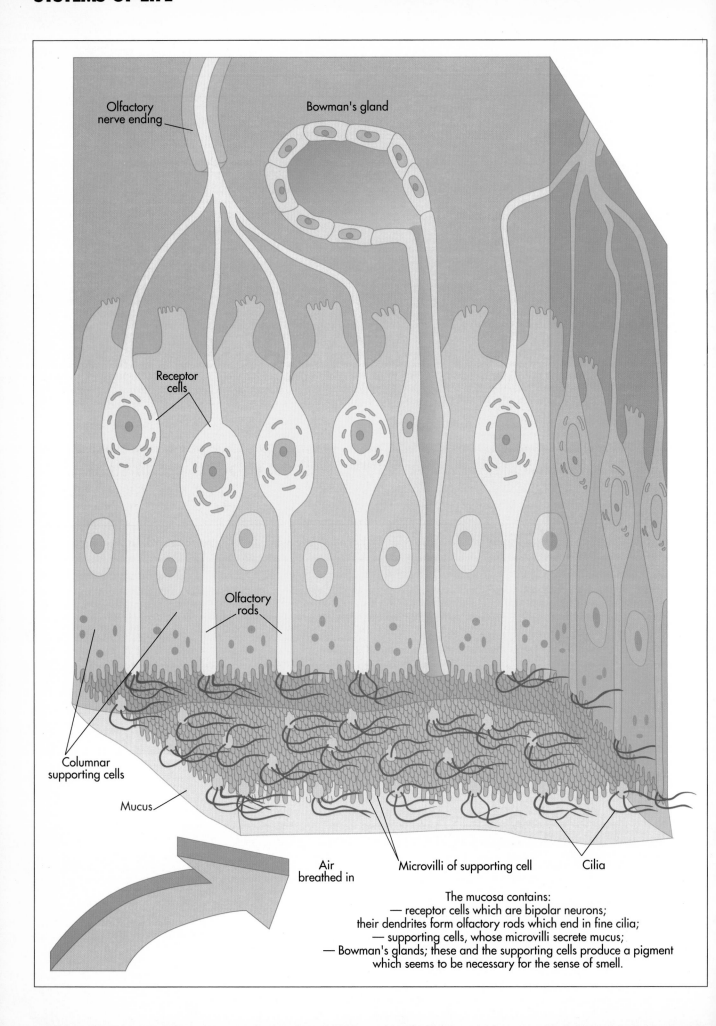

Olfactory nerve ending

Bowman's gland

Receptor cells

Olfactory rods

Columnar supporting cells

Mucus

Air breathed in

Microvilli of supporting cell

Cilia

The mucosa contains:
— receptor cells which are bipolar neurons;
their dendrites form olfactory rods which end in fine cilia;
— supporting cells, whose microvilli secrete mucus;
— Bowman's glands; these and the supporting cells produce a pigment
which seems to be necessary for the sense of smell.

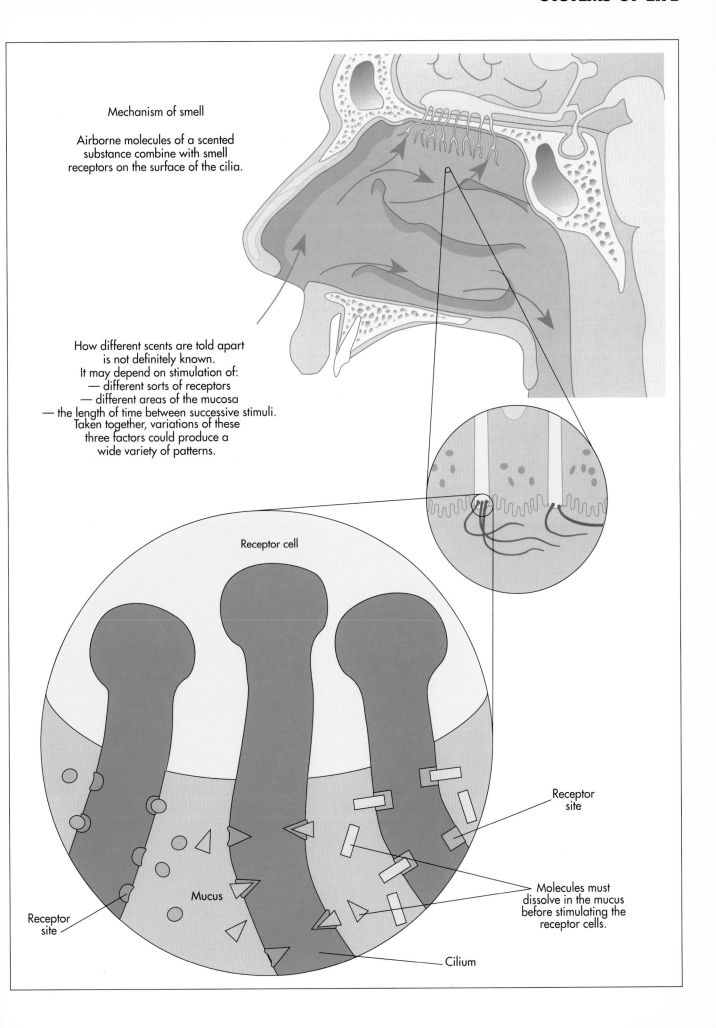

Mechanism of smell

Airborne molecules of a scented substance combine with smell receptors on the surface of the cilia.

How different scents are told apart is not definitely known. It may depend on stimulation of:
— different sorts of receptors
— different areas of the mucosa
— the length of time between successive stimuli. Taken together, variations of these three factors could produce a wide variety of patterns.

Receptor cell

Receptor site

Receptor site

Molecules must dissolve in the mucus before stimulating the receptor cells.

Mucus

Cilium

The sense of smell is transmitted by the olfactory (1st cranial) nerve and its connections.
Information about substances that irritate the nose, like onions or ammonia,
is transmitted to the brain along the 5th (trigeminal) nerve.

Stimulation of smell receptors sets up an action potential, and the resulting nerve impulse is carried
along the nerve fibres through the cribriform plate to the olfactory bulb.
From here information about smell is relayed to the temporal lobe of the cerebral cortex.
There are also connections with the hypothalamus, and the limbic system
which is concerned with learning, memory and emotion.

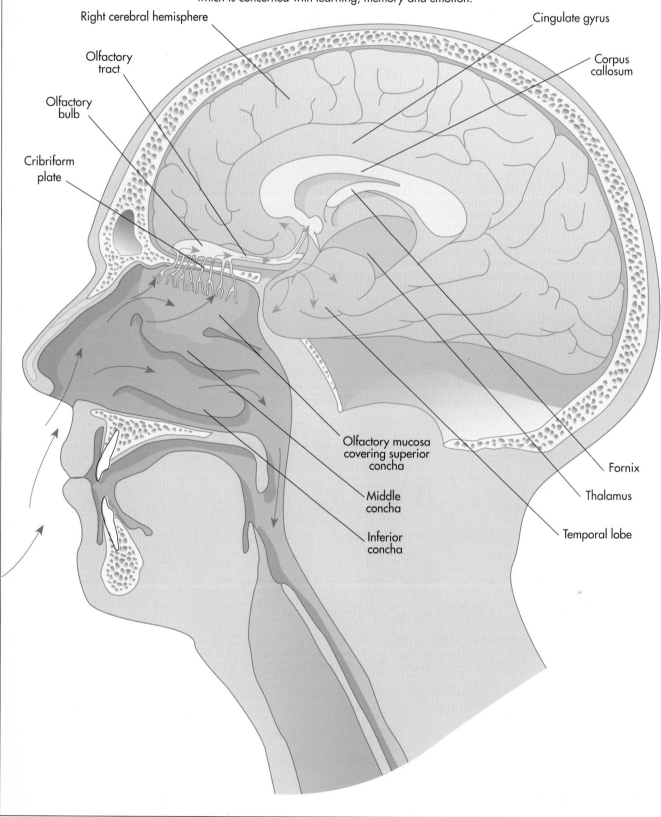

Right cerebral hemisphere

Olfactory tract

Olfactory bulb

Cribriform plate

Cingulate gyrus

Corpus callosum

Olfactory mucosa covering superior concha

Middle concha

Inferior concha

Fornix

Thalamus

Temporal lobe